WITHDRAWN

21st Century Skills Library

COOL SCIENCE CAREERS

ARCHITECTS

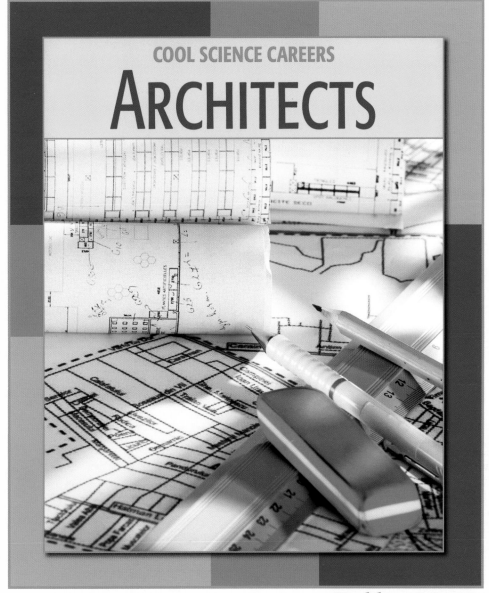

Kathleen Manatt

Cherry Lake Publishing
Ann Arbor, Michigan

Published in the United States of America by Cherry Lake Publishing
Ann Arbor, MI
www.cherrylakepublishing.com

Photo Credits: Page 18, University of Washington Libraries, Special Collections, FAR017;
Page 24, Photo Courtesy of Martin Schall

Library of Congress Cataloging-in-Publication Data
Manatt, Kathleen G
  Architects / by Kathleen Manatt.
     p. cm. — (Cool science careers)
  Includes bibliographical references.
  ISBN-13: 978-1-60279-052-0 (hardcover)   978-1-60279-078-0 (pbk.)
  ISBN-10: 1-60279-052-3 (hardcover)   1-60279-078-7 (pbk.)
  1. Architects—Juvenile literature. 2. Architecture—Vocational guidance—Juvenile literature. I.
Title. II. Series.
  NA2555.M36 2007
  720.23—dc22   2007005621

Cherry Lake Publishing would like to acknowledge the work of
The Partnership for 21st Century Skills.
Please visit www.21stcenturyskills.org for more information.

TABLE of CONTENTS

CHAPTER ONE

THEN AND NOW

Egypt's pyramids are some of the most famous buildings in the world, and thousands of tourists travel to Egypt every year to see them.

Who built the pyramids at Giza, Egypt? We know they were built about

4,000 years ago as burial chambers for three Egyptian pharaohs, or kings.

But somebody had to figure out where to place the pyramids. (On a sturdy

rock plateau on the west side of the Nile River, where they wouldn't sink into the sand.) Someone had to decide what kinds and sizes of stone to use. (They used limestone on the outside and granite on much of the inside.)

The largest pyramid is called the Great Pyramid. It was originally more than 481 feet (147 meters) tall. It is made of more than 2.3 million blocks of stone and weighs 5.75 million tons (5.22 million metric tons).

Some people think that one of the pharaoh's advisors, a man named Hemon, was the architect of the Great Pyramid. If so, he was one of the world's first architects. An architect is a person who plans and oversees a building's construction.

Learning & Innovation Skills

The original entrance to the Great Pyramid was about 59 feet (18 meters) above ground level. Why do you think the architect made the doorway so high? Hint: Think about burglars.

Becoming an Architect

Almost certainly, the architects of the pyramids learned most of their craft through "on the job training." There was little formal schooling for anybody.

Today things are different. Future architects study art and math. Math is required to make many of the decisions about the design and construction of buildings. Architects go to college for five years and then work as interns for three more years. Then they must pass a state exam.

Math is needed to determine key elements in a building's plans, including the amount of weight a specific wall can support.

CHAPTER TWO

ALL IN A DAY'S WORK

Architects often don't get to choose where their creations will be built. It

is quite common for a prospective client to come to an architect with an

idea in mind and the land for it already purchased. The client probably has

*Designing large office buildings usually requires large teams of
architects, each one of which may work on a different part.*

a budget in mind, too. It is the architect's job to mesh these three factors together. Sometimes this is easy, and sometimes it is not.

The architect begins by listening intently to the client and then making sketches. Doing this gives both parties a better understanding of what the project may involve. Sometimes the sketches are revised many times before the final plan evolves.

A key issue is the budget. Too often, the client has great ideas but does not have a budget to match. The architect must come up with a list of costs for specific items. The client can then decide what to eliminate.

8

Architectural plans must describe everything from what material will cover the outside to how many light switches there will be.

The architect will also meet with specialized engineers to work out

plans for heating, cooling, water, and electrical systems, for example.

These engineers can help make the finished building work more efficiently

and be less costly to operate. The engineers' suggestions may require

changes in the basic plan that the architect will have to discuss with the

21st Century Content

Cities around the world have rules and requirements for building that have to be met. The rules in Singapore differ from those in Ottawa. In all cases, many licenses need to be gotten before construction can begin. Among other things, these rules, requirements, and licenses help ensure that the completed building will be safe to use.

client. Sometimes, suggested changes may cost more initially but will save money later. If so, the budget may have to be adjusted, too.

Now the architect and the client can meet with the general contractor to go over the plans in detail. The contractor may point out potential problems, and the plans may need to be revised once again.

So far, the project has mostly been talk, but that is about to change. Based on the final plan, materials can start to be ordered, including wood, steel, cement, nails, screws, windows, doors, sinks, toilets, air conditioners, furnaces, carpet, lights—the list may seem endless.

The architect has to be sure that the building plans call for just the right sizes and amounts of everything. Too little of something, and construction will be halted. Too much of something, and money may be wasted. Everything has to be the correct size, too. What if the opening for the door turns out to be two inches smaller than the door itself?

Once construction begins, the architect will visit the building site often and continue to meet with the client. The architect will also regularly check on the building budget and materials status. Sometimes, prices change. Other times, some

The construction of a very large building
can take two years or more.

item may suddenly be unavailable. Then the

architect is pressured to come up with a brilliant

solution quickly.

The architect may also be on hand when building

inspectors arrive. These people check on progress and

make sure that proper materials are being used and

construction techniques are OK. A mistake could cost

money, time, or even lives. For example,

14 workers died constructing the Empire State

Building. If a building inspector objects, all

construction may halt. So making sure that

everything is being done correctly is very important

to the architect and everyone else.

Architects often work on several projects at once. However, these projects may not be in the same city or even the same country. When such things occur, the architect has to also be a good traveler and time juggler.

As the project is completed, the architect will tour the building to make sure that everything is done correctly and meets the client's needs. Then it's time to relax and enjoy the results!

CHAPTER THREE

SOME FAMOUS ARCHITECTS

*Construction of Casa Milà began in 1905 and took
five years to complete. The famous apartment
building has wavy walls on the inside, too.*

A most unusual architect was born in Spain in the 1800s. His name

was Antonio Gaudí, and his buildings are most unusual, too. Take the

Casa Milà, an apartment building in Barcelona, Spain. To many people,

the building looks like it's melting. When Casa Milà was built in the early

1900s, many people thought it was ugly, but now it is a city landmark.

The Roeblings

It took a whole family to build New York City's famous Brooklyn Bridge. John Roebling designed the bridge in 1867, but he died in 1869. The responsibility for construction fell to his son, Washington. Then disaster struck again. Washington was paralyzed in a work accident in 1872. His wife, Emily, became his eyes and ears on the building site for the next 11 years of construction. When the bridge officially opened on May 24, 1883, Emily Roebling was the first person to cross.

Frank Lloyd Wright

When Frank Lloyd Wright began designing

houses in the late 1800s, most people wanted the

fussy Victorian style with towers and turrets.

However, Wright lived in the Midwest, and he

designed houses that reflected the sweeping prairies

of that area. He built houses that were long and low

and "swept" across their settings. Wright was also

very particular about what went into his houses. He

even designed the lamps and flower vases.

Frank Lloyd Wright was short, and the doorways he designed were not very high. Many tall people today bump their heads on them. If Wright were designing a house for you, what would you tell him to do about the doorways?

CHAPTER FOUR

WHEN THINGS GO BAD

People living around Puget Sound in Washington State had long wanted

a bridge across the Tacoma Narrows. They finally got it in July of 1940.

The bridge was solidly built but did not allow wind to pass through the

*The remains of the Tacoma Narrows Bridge still
sit on the bottom of Puget Sound today.*

roadbed. And Tacoma Narrows is a windy place! On November 7, 1940, a fierce wind caused the roadbed to sway violently. Soon the bridge collapsed into the river below. It took ten years to build a new, safer one.

The *Titanic*

On April 10, 1912, the fabulous *Titanic* set sail on its first voyage. It was the biggest and most luxurious ship of its time. However, it carried lifeboats for only about half the people aboard. *Titanic* used new technology that was supposed to make it unsinkable. On April 14, the ship hit an iceberg and was torn apart. More than 1,500 people died. One of them, Thomas Andrews, Jr., was one of the ship's designers.

Life & Career Skills

People are accountable for their actions and decisions. Who was accountable for the *Titanic* disaster? Was it Andrews and his company and their new technology? Was it the people who decided to have too few lifeboats? Or was it the captain who kept the ship speeding through the dark waters even though there were warnings of icebergs in the area?

The Sydney Opera House

The opera house in Sydney, Australia, is one of the world's most famous buildings. Jørn Utzon of Denmark was the architect. Government leaders in Australia pushed for a quick start on construction because they feared that public opinion would turn against the cost of the project.

The famous sail-shaped roof is made of 2,194 pre-cast concrete sections that are covered with more than one million tiles.

Construction began in 1959 but was soon almost a year behind schedule. Work had begun before the engineering and construction problems of the revolutionary design had been worked out.

In 1965, new government leaders began arguing with Utzon about the mounting costs. He resigned in 1966. The building was finally finished in 1973 but cost much, much, much more than planned. Who is to blame for this? Architect Utzon, who created the fantastic design? Or the government leaders, who had forced construction to begin before the plans were finished?

Life & Career Skills

Making sound financial decisions is important to governments as well as businesses and individuals. As the cost of the Sydney Opera House mounted, government leaders failed to make the decisions necessary to curb costs or speed completion. In the end the cost overruns caused a scandal.

The Walt Disney Concert Hall

Frank Gehry is one of the most famous architects in the world today, and rightly so. Some of his buildings are covered with stainless steel and have wildly curving walls. The Walt Disney Concert Hall is one of them.

The outside of the Walt Disney Concert Hall is covered with 12,500 pieces of steel. No two pieces are the same size or shape.

However, when the building was finished in 2003, it immediately began to cause problems. Light reflected off some of the shiny curved sides. It started fires in trash bins and melted plastic traffic cones.

Gehry and his team had to figure out a solution. First, they determined the exact walls that were causing problems. Then they tried out various ways of making the walls just a little less shiny. They sampled liquids that could be poured over the shiny surfaces to dull the shine. However, they finally had the offending walls gently sanded so some of the very shiny surfaces reflected less light. Problem solved.

21st Century Content

Frank Gehry and his team took responsibility for the problems the building's design caused. The information they gathered informed several future projects. To see several of Gehry's projects, go to http://www.pritzkerprize.com/gehry/gehrypg.htm

CHAPTER FIVE

INTO THE FUTURE

*This revolutionary building in southern California produces
some of the electricity it needs with a special reflective "skin."*

Making Electricity

Whether it is a home or an office skyscraper, almost all buildings require electricity to operate. It is needed to run lights, computers, elevators, even plumbing! Southern California has a new 10-story office building that makes its own electricity. The architects used computers to design an outside "skin" for the building made of special glass panels. The glass panels produce electricity from the huge amounts of sunlight that hit the building.

Why wouldn't this type of new building be as suitable for Seattle, Washington, as it would be for Phoenix, Arizona? *Hint*: Think about the climate.

Learning & Innovation Skills

Innovation and inventiveness are essential for future development. Computers are now used in many types of design projects, from airplanes and skyscrapers to books, homes, and sewer lines. Through modeling and similar programs, computers allow architects to see how concepts will look—and more importantly—work when completed.

Use that Water!

Rainwater usually runs off buildings and directly into city sewers. However, architects in rainy Seattle, Washington, had a better idea. They designed an 8-story office building that collects about 1.4 million gallons (5.3 million liters) of rainwater every year. It collects on the roof. Then it is filtered and used in the building's many toilets. The system supplies about two-thirds of the water needed for the toilets and has cut the building's "flushing budget" by more than 60 percent.

Use It, Don't Burn It

Designing buildings that are warm in winter and cool in summer is an important goal for architects. Today, some architects are finding new ways to use straw. Usually this straw is burned and causes a great deal of air pollution. However, architects now are using the straw for insulation in walls. Sometimes the straw is made into the walls themselves. The straw keeps the buildings warm in winter and cool in summer—and stops air pollution, too!

Straw bale insulation is cost effective to use and easily available.

*The Louvre in Paris, France, has been one of the world's
most famous museums for more than 200 years.*

Bringing the Past into the Present

The Louvre in Paris, France, is one of the world's great museums.

However, by the 1980s, the building needed a new entrance for the

millions of tourists who visit every year. The president of France hired

Chinese-American I. M. Pei to be the architect.

Pei created a revolutionary design that brought the old—a pyramid—

into today. Since the museum includes hundreds of pieces from ancient

Egypt, the new entrance is the perfect shape!

More than eight million people visited the Louvre Museum in 2006.

GLOSSARY

architect (AHR-ki-tekt) person who plans, designs, and oversees a building's construction

client (KLAHY-uhnt) customer

construction (kuhn-STRUHK-shuhn) process of erecting a building

design (di-ZAHYN) artistic plan or pattern

iceberg (AHYS-burg) massive, floating piece of ice that has broken off a glacier. Usually only a very small part of an iceberg can be seen above the water.

insulation (in-suh-LEY-shuhn) material used to slow the transfer of heat through walls

pyramid (PIR-uh-mid) building with a square base and four triangular sides that slant upwards to a point

site (sahyt) place where a building is located

turrets (TUR-its, TUHR-) small towers or tower-shaped projections on a building

FOR MORE INFORMATION

Books

Glenn, Patricia Brown. *Discover America's Favorite Architects.*
New York: Preservation Press, 1996.

Glenn, Patricia Brown. *Under Every Roof: A Kid's Style
and Field Guide to the Architecture of American Houses.*
New York: Preservation Press, 1993.

Macaulay, David. *Castle.* Boston: Houghton Mifflin, 1977.

Macaulay, David. *Pyramid.* Boston: Houghton Mifflin, 1975.

Macaulay, David. *Unbuilding.* Boston: Houghton Mifflin, 1980.

McCall, Henrietta. *Pyramid.* New York: Franklin Watts, 1999.

McDonough, Yona Zeldis. *Frank Lloyd Wright.*
New York: Chelsea House, 1992.

Parker, Steven. *I Wonder Why Tunnels Are Round and Other Questions
About Building.* New York: Kingfisher Publications, Plc., 1995.

Steele, Philip. *I Wonder Why the Pyramids Were Built.*
New York: Kingfisher Publications, Plc., 1995.

Other Media

Building Big: "Bridges." VHS. WGBH, Boston, 2000.

Modern Marvels: "The Empire State Building."
DVD. The History Channel, 1994.

Modern Marvels: "Engineering Disasters." DVD. The History Channel, 2005.

Modern Marvels: "Gothic Cathedrals." DVD. The History Channel, 1998.

Nova: "Super Bridge." VHS. WGBH, Boston, 1997.

INDEX

ABOUT THE AUTHOR

Kathleen Manatt is a long-time writer, editor, and publisher of books for children. Many of her books have been about faraway places, which she likes to visit. She grew up in Illinois, Iowa, New Jersey, and California, and lived in Chicago for many years as an adult. She has climbed pyramids in Mexico, ridden elephants in Thailand, and toured the fjords of Norway. She has also visited Moscow, Lisbon, Paris, Geneva, London, Madrid, Edinburgh, and Barcelona. She now lives in Austin, Texas.